D1358735

# THE HUMAN BODY

### SALLY MORGAN

## KINGFISHER
### NEW YORK

**KINGFISHER**
LONDON & NEW YORK

Copyright © Kingfisher 2001
Published in the United States by Kingfisher,
175 Fifth Ave., New York, NY 10010
Kingfisher is an imprint of Macmillan Children's
Books, London.

Distributed in the U.S. and Canada by Macmillan,
175 Fifth Ave., New York, NY 10010

LIBRARY OF CONGRESS CATALOGING-IN-PUBLICATION DATA
Morgan, Sally.
  The human body / Sally Morgan.—1st ed.
    p.  cm.—(Young discoverers)
  Includes index.
  Summary: Introduces the parts of the body and their
functions and discusses the importance of a balanced diet
and exercise. Includes related activities and experiments.
1. Human physiology—Juvenile literature. [1. Human
physiology. 2. Body, Human.] I. Title. II. Series.
Q37.M69434   1996
612—dc20  96-14B11  CIP AC

ISBN: 978-0-7534-5501-2

Kingfisher books are available for special
promotions and premiums. For details contact:
Special Markets Department, Macmillan,
175 Fifth Avenue, New York, NY 10010.

For more information, please visit
www.kingfisherbooks.com

First American Edition 1996
Printed in China
10 9 8
8TR/0913/WKT/(RNB)/128MA/F

Consultant: Brian Ward
Cover design: John Jamieson
Illustrations: Peter Bull pp. 7 (bot.), 9 (bot. right), 13 (bot. right),
16 (bot.), 23 (top),  25 (top & bot. left), 27 (top), 30 (bot. right);
Joanne Cowne pp. 8 (bot. right), 10, 14 (left); Richard Draper
p. 19 (right); Ryz Hajdal pp. 30 (top), 31; Nick Hall pp. 5 (bot.
& right), 13 (center), 15 (top left), 20 (left), 22 (left), 28 (left),
30 (left); Karen Hiscock pp. 18 (center), 20 (center); Ian Jackson
pp. 12 (top), 13 (top), 25 (bot. right); Ruth Lindsay p. 17 (center); Jenny Mumford pp. 9 (left), 16 (bot. left), 23 (bot. left); Chris Orr p.
25 (center right); Eric Robson pp. 26 (center), 26–27, 28–29,
29 (top right & left); Mike Saunders pp. 4 (top) 21, 28 (top);
Shirley Tourret pp. 23 (bot. right), 24 (top); Richard Ward pp. 7
(top & center), 8 (left & top), 11, 15 (top right), 17 (top & bot.),
18 (left), 19 (left), 24 (left); Steve Weston pp. 4–5, 6, 14 (center). Photographs: Bruce Coleman p. 19 (John Murray);
Ecoscene pp. 9, 10; National Medical Slide Bank p. 6; NHPA
p. 4; Panos pp. 15 (Jenny Hartley), 27 (Wang Gang Feng);
Science Photo Library p. 16 (Aaron Polliack); Supersport p. 31
(Eileen Langley); Zefa p. 22.

# About This Book

This book looks at how your body works and what it is made of. It explains why you need a healthy diet and plenty of exercise to keep your body fit. It also suggests lots of experiments and things to look for.

You should be able to find nearly everything you need for the experiments in your home or in a local hardware store.

### Activity Hints
- Before you begin an experiment, read through the instructions carefully and collect all the things you need.
- When you have finished, put everything away and wash your hands.
- Start a special notebook so that you can keep a record of what you do in each experiment and the things you find out.

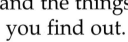

# Contents

 **What Are We Made Of?** 4

 **The Skeleton** 6

 **Teeth** 8

 **A Healthy Diet** 10

 **Digestion** 12

 **The Waterworks** 14

 **Heart and Circulation** 16

 **Breathing** 18

 **The Nervous System** 20

 **The Senses** 22

 **The Skin** 24

 **Inheritance** 26

 **Growing Up** 28

 **Keeping Fit** 30

 **Index** 32

# What Are We Made Of?

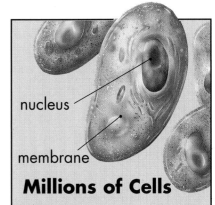

Your body is two-thirds water.

The rest is made up of about 50 billion tiny cells—the basic building blocks of life. These vary in shape and size and carry out different jobs. For example, red blood cells carry oxygen, and nerve cells pass messages to and from the brain. Cells have only a limited lifetime, so they have to be repaired or replaced when they wear out. Groups of the same type of cell form body tissue such as skin or muscle. Groups of different types of tissue make up organs such as the heart and the lungs. Each organ has a particular job to do in the body.

nucleus

membrane

## Millions of Cells

Cells cannot be seen with the naked eye, but they can be examined under a microscope. They have a membrane around the outside and contain a nucleus, or control center.

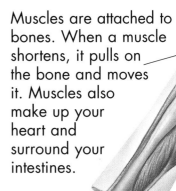

Muscles are attached to bones. When a muscle shortens, it pulls on the bone and moves it. Muscles also make up your heart and surround your intestines.

## Mammals

Humans, like mice, belong to a group of animals called mammals. They share several similar characteristics. Mammals have mammary glands, which allow females to produce milk for their young. Mammals also have a constant body temperature, which for humans is 98.6°F (37°C).

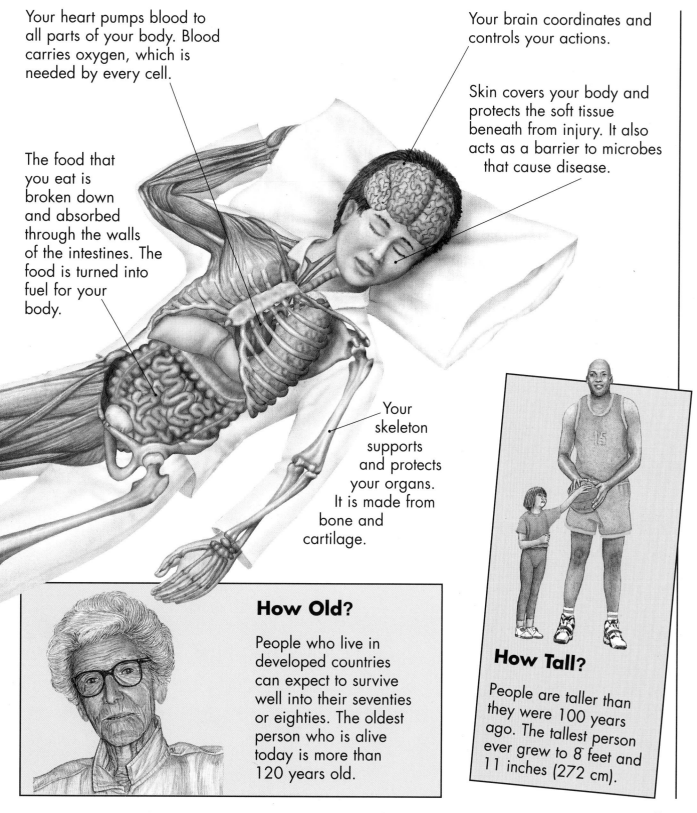

Your heart pumps blood to all parts of your body. Blood carries oxygen, which is needed by every cell.

Your brain coordinates and controls your actions.

Skin covers your body and protects the soft tissue beneath from injury. It also acts as a barrier to microbes that cause disease.

The food that you eat is broken down and absorbed through the walls of the intestines. The food is turned into fuel for your body.

Your skeleton supports and protects your organs. It is made from bone and cartilage.

## How Old?

People who live in developed countries can expect to survive well into their seventies or eighties. The oldest person who is alive today is more than 120 years old.

## How Tall?

People are taller than they were 100 years ago. The tallest person ever grew to 8 feet and 11 inches (272 cm).

5

# The Skeleton

The skeleton is the hardest and strongest part of your body. Without it, you could not stand up or move. The skeleton protects your organs, and the muscles that move your limbs are attached to it. The spine supports your body. It is made up of a column of small bones called vertebrae. These are separated by small rubbery disks of cartilage that cushion the bones and allow the spine to bend. Joints allow other bones to move.

skull

radius

ulna

humerus

collarbone

shoulder blade

breastbone

ribs

spine

hip

femur

kneecap

fibula

tibia

toes

fingers

### X rays

Doctors use X rays to take photographs of bones inside a patient's body. This X ray shows a broken arm.

The human skeleton is made up of 206 bones. The largest are the thigh bones, or femurs. The smallest are three tiny bones inside the ear.

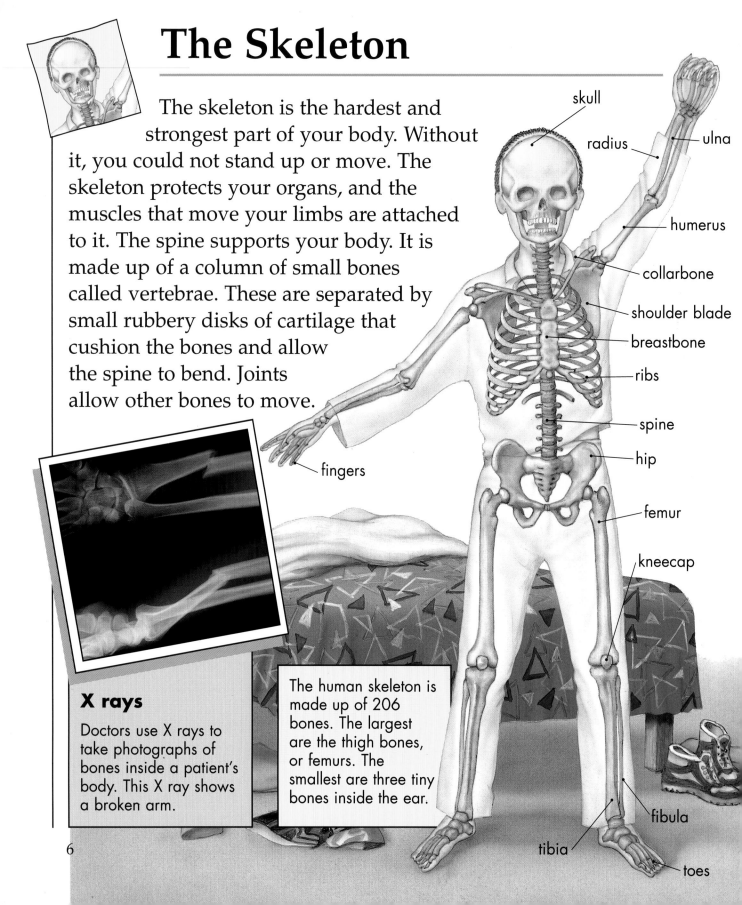

# Do it yourself

## Muscles work in pairs. One contracts, while the other relaxes.

**1.** Take two lengths of wood. Ask an adult to help you join the ends using a hinge. This will be an elbow.

**2.** Attach four hooks to the wood, as shown. Use short lengths of string to attach rubber bands between the hooks.

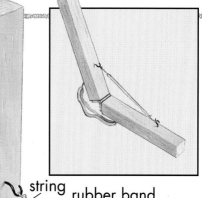
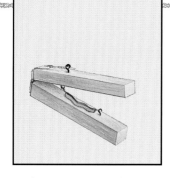

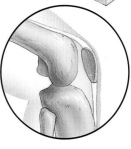
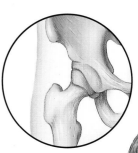

string
rubber band "biceps"
hinge "elbow"
rubber band "triceps"
hook

**3.** The top rubber band acts as the biceps muscle and the one underneath is the triceps muscle. When you bend the two pieces of wood at the elbow, the triceps muscle stretch and the biceps shorten.

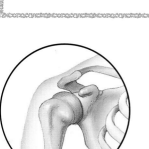
shoulder

hip

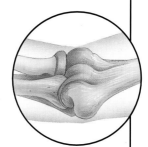
knee

elbow

## Joints

Shoulder and hip joints are called ball-and-socket joints because the upper arm bone and the thigh bone end in a smooth ball that swivels in a hollow socket. This type of joint allows movement in all directions. Elbow and knee joints are called hinge joints because they work like the hinge on a door. These joints move only in one direction, and back again. The bones of a joint are held in place by stretchy ligaments. A smooth layer of cartilage over the ends acts as a cushion against shock and stops bones from wearing away as they rub against each other.

# Teeth

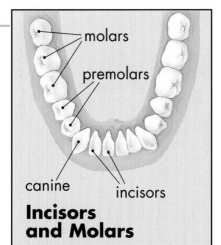

The first set of 20 teeth, called baby teeth, start to appear within a few months of birth. Under the baby teeth, deep in the gums, are the permanent teeth. The first permanent teeth appear at about six years of age. They push out the baby teeth as they grow. An adult has 32 teeth. Beneath the tough outer covering of enamel is dentine, which makes up most of the tooth. It is softer than enamel and is easily damaged by decay. Deep in the middle is the pulp cavity, which contains nerves and blood vessels.

## Incisors and Molars

The sharp incisors at the front are for cutting food, and the canines next to them are for tearing food. Premolars and molars are the large, rough teeth at the back that are used for grinding food.

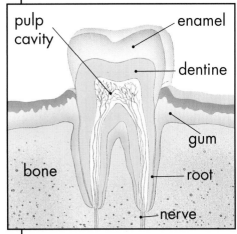

A colorless, sticky layer called plaque forms over your teeth. Unless you brush your teeth correctly, it hardens to form tartar, a tough layer that is difficult to remove and eventually leads to gum disease and tooth decay.

## Avoid Teeth Like These!

Bacteria in your mouth produce acids that dissolve away the surface of a tooth's enamel and cause decay. A toothache starts when decay reaches the nerves. A dentist will remove the decay and replace it with a filling of gray amalgam (a mixture of metals), or white plastic, which blends in better with the tooth.

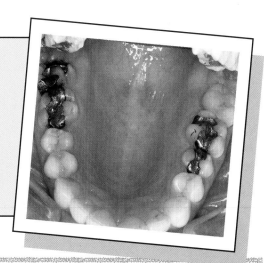

# Do it yourself

**Some teeth are designed to bite off food, and others are better for grinding. The teeth you use to bite off food have sharp edges. Those for grinding are larger with a ridged surface.**

**1.** Using a mirror, look at the teeth in your mouth. How many teeth have you got? Are they baby teeth or permanent teeth? Can you name them?

**2.** Take a bite of raw carrot and chew it. Which teeth did you use to bite off a piece? Which teeth did you use to chew the carrot? Did your tongue help?

### 👁 Eye-Spy

How many of your teeth have fillings? Carry out a survey to find out how many fillings your friends have. Which teeth are most usually filled? Do your parents have more or fewer fillings than you?

9

# A Healthy Diet

Your body needs a mixture of foods that contain different nutrients. Carbohydrates and fats produce energy. Bread, potatoes, and cereals are rich in carbohydrates. Dairy products and meat contain fat. You need protein for growth and to repair cells. Meat, eggs, and beans provide protein. Your body needs minerals and vitamins, too. Calcium, also found in milk and cheese, helps build strong teeth and bones. Iron is needed for red blood cells.

## Vitamins

Vitamins are named by letters. Vegetables and fruit are good sources of vitamin C. Milk and cheese provide vitamins A and D. Grains such as rice and cereals provide vitamin B.

What do you eat for breakfast? Most likely, you have a bowl of cereal with milk, and maybe some toast. Somebody living in Indonesia might have rice mixed with vegetables and topped with a fried egg. Both meals are a healthy start to the day.

# Do it yourself

**Try this test to identify foods that contain starch, a carbohydrate found in plant foods.**

**1.** Collect a selection of foods such as a cookie, an apple, cheese, and a potato. Grind up a small sample of one of them.

**2.** Add a small amount of water and mix well. Set aside for a few minutes and then pour the liquid into a small container.

**3.** Add a drop of iodine. If starch is present, the liquid will turn blue-black.

**4.** Repeat this for each food. Which ones contain starch?

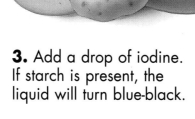

## Vegetarians

People who follow a vegetarian diet do not eat meat. Their meals are based on vegetables, especially legumes (beans and peas), often with some eggs, milk, and cheese for protein.

## Junk Food

Sweetened drinks, potato chips, hamburgers, and french fries are called "junk food." They are convenient—but not very healthy. They contain lots of fat and carbohydrates.

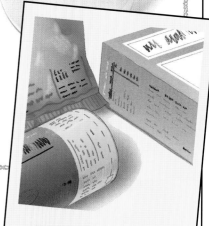

## 👁 Eye-Spy

Look for the list of contents on packaged foods. Some foods contain preservatives, or are given artificial color and taste. There may also be numbers for energy (calories), fat, and protein.

# Digestion

Food provides energy for your body and helps you to grow. When you swallow, chewed food mixed with saliva passes to your stomach and intestines. Digestive juices, which contain chemicals called enzymes, surround the food and break it down so that it can pass through the walls of the intestine into the blood system. Once digestion is complete, all that is left is a small quantity of feces. This contains the bits of food you cannot digest, and it passes out of your body when you go to the bathroom.

## Salivation

When we see, smell, or think about food, glands under the tongue start to release saliva. This helps to break down food for the digestive process. Animals salivate, too. You may have seen a dog drool when it is given some food.

## Do it yourself

**Saliva lubricates food so that it is easy to swallow.**

**1.** Chew a small cube of dry bread without swallowing.

**2.** As the bread becomes mushy, you should start to detect a sweet taste in your mouth.

**3.** Repeat this with a piece of apple or cheese. Is there any difference?

### How It Works

The enzymes in your saliva break down starch into sugar. This produces the sweet taste in your mouth. This only happens with foods such as bread, which contain cooked starch.

## Special Stomachs

Plants contain a tough material called cellulose, which cannot be digested by humans. A cow's large stomach contains bacteria that can digest cellulose. To help digestion, the cow brings up the food and chews it a second time.

👁 **Eye-Spy**

Food provides energy for daily activities such as walking and running. Make a list of all the things you do during the day that require your body to use energy.

Your digestive system is about 30 feet (9 m) long. Food passes from your mouth to your stomach, where it is stored for up to four hours. Food may take several days to pass through the digestive system. Muscles in the walls of the intestines squeeze to push the food along.

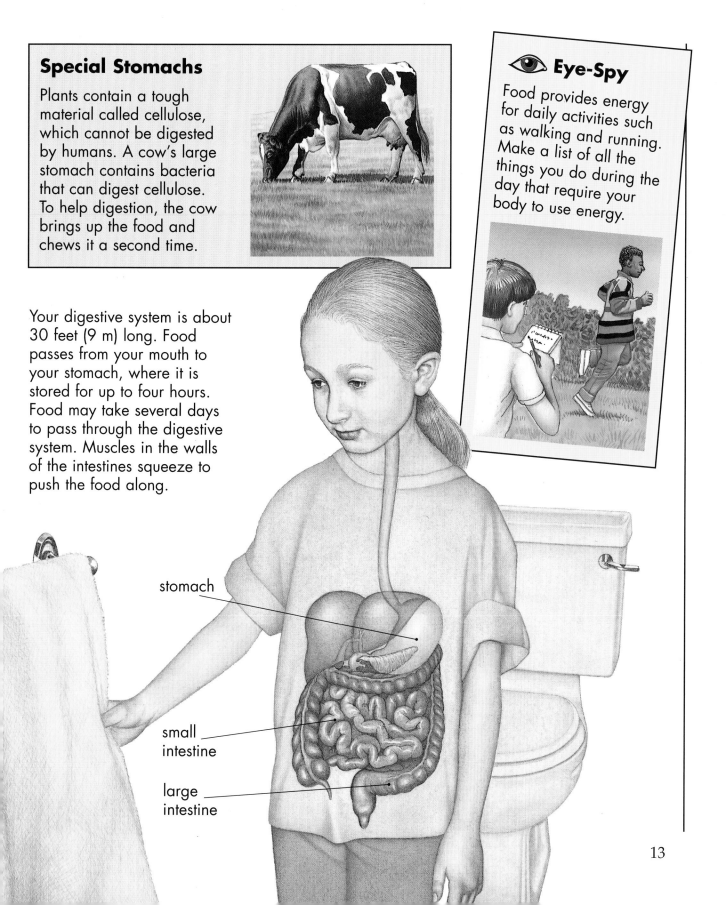

stomach

small intestine

large intestine

13

# The Waterworks

Your kidneys filter out wastes and excess water from your blood after food has been digested. The waste materials become a liquid called urine. Urine travels down two tubes called ureters to your bladder, where it is stored. When the sphincter muscle on your bladder relaxes, the urine flows down another tube called the urethra and out of your body. Your kidneys also help to control the amount of fluid in your body. If you drink a lot of water, your body has to get rid of some, so it produces extra urine.

Each of us has two kidneys. Every day, 400 gallons (1,500 l) of blood circulate through your kidneys.

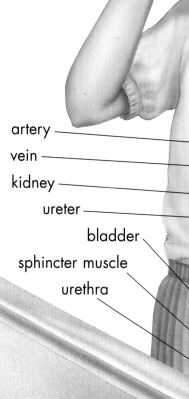

artery
vein
kidney
ureter
bladder
sphincter muscle
urethra

## Hot and Thirsty

During exercise, your skin sweats to help keep you cool. This water has to be replaced, so your brain tells you that you need water by making you feel thirsty.

# Do it yourself

**You can make a very simple filter to show how a kidney works.**

**1.** Use a paper coffee filter, or fold a piece of paper towel into a cone shape. Put the filter into a plastic funnel. Place the funnel in a container.

**2.** Grind up some chalk and mix the powder in water so that it is very cloudy. Pour the cloudy water into the filter.

**3.** The water that drips from the filter is much clearer than the water that went into the filter. The filter in your kidney is similar. It lets some of the water and all of the waste through, but keeps back the valuable blood cells.

## Why Do Babies Need Diapers?

Babies have no control over the moment when urine passes out of their bladder. They have to learn how to use the sphincter muscle.

## Water to Drink

A person can survive for many days without food but will die within two days without water. In parts of Africa where it is hot and there is not much rain, people often have to travel long distances to find enough clean water to drink. During a severe drought, many thousands of people can die.

# Heart and Circulation

Blood is circulated all around your body through a system of blood vessels. At the center of the blood system is your heart—pumping constantly day and night. Arteries carry blood from your heart to all parts of your body. Veins bring blood from which oxygen has been removed back to your heart. Blood carries oxygen from the lungs and food from the intestines to the cells, and picks up carbon dioxide and other waste materials from the cells.

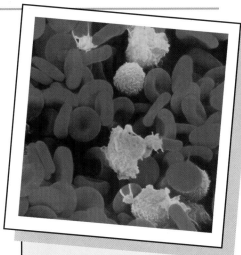

## Blood Cells

Blood is made up of plasma and blood cells. Red cells carry oxygen and white cells protect your body from disease.

# Do it yourself

**Your pulse tells how fast your heart is beating.**

**1.** Take your pulse while you are resting. Count the number of pulses, or beats, you can feel in one minute.

**2.** Now run up and down some stairs.

**3.** Take your pulse again. By how much has your pulse rate increased?

**4.** Wait five minutes and measure your pulse again. Has it returned to normal?

## How It Works

When you exercise, your muscles need oxygen. Your heart beats more quickly in order to pump blood to the muscles. Your pulse may increase from 60–75 beats to over 100 per minute.

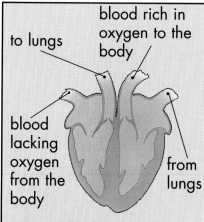

to lungs

blood rich in oxygen to the body

blood lacking oxygen from the body

from lungs

## The Heart

Your heart is two pumps working side by side. Blood from your body enters the right side and is pumped to the lungs. Blood from the lungs returns to the left side and is pumped to your body.

Your body has 60,000 miles (100,000 km) of blood vessels containing nearly 2 gallons (7 l) of blood. Arteries and veins are linked by tiny capillaries.

blood

fatty deposits

## Blocked Arteries

If arteries in the heart become clogged with fatty deposits, the flow of blood is reduced and part of the heart muscle may not get enough oxygen. The result is often a heart attack.

platelets

red blood cell

## Clotting Blood

If you cut yourself, small cells in your blood called platelets form a network of fibers across the cut. Red blood cells become trapped in the net and harden to form a scab.

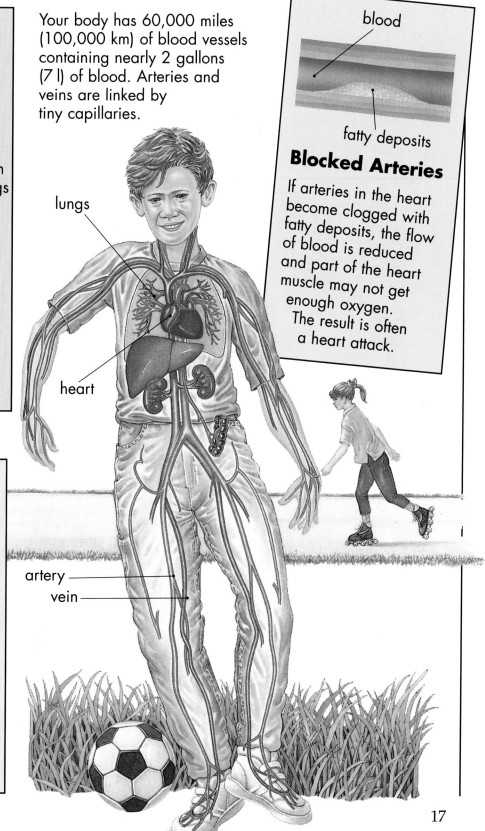

lungs

heart

artery

vein

17

# Breathing

Every four or five seconds, you take a fresh breath of air into your lungs. When you breathe in, your chest expands as your lungs fill with air. Air contains oxygen, which the blood cells need to release the energy locked up in food. The cells produce a waste gas called carbon dioxide. This is picked up by the blood and carried back to your lungs. When you breathe out, the air that leaves your lungs contains much less oxygen, but an increased amount of carbon dioxide.

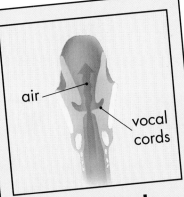

air

vocal cords

## How we speak

When you speak, muscles in your neck bring the vocal cords in your larynx close together. Air leaving your lungs is forced through the cords, which vibrate and produce a sound.

The trachea leads from the back of the throat into the chest and then divides into two narrower tubes called bronchi. These carry air into the lungs. Beneath the lungs there is a muscle called the diaphragm, which moves down when you breathe in, helping to suck air into the lungs, and up when you breathe out again.

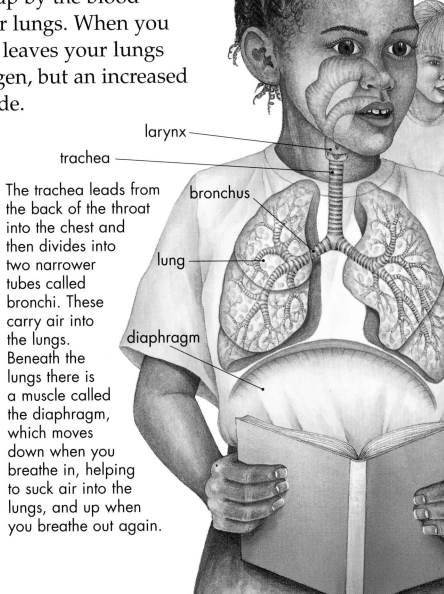

larynx

trachea

bronchus

lung

diaphragm

## Breathing Under Water

Divers take compressed air with them in a special cylinder. They use a mask and breathing apparatus so that they can breathe normally.

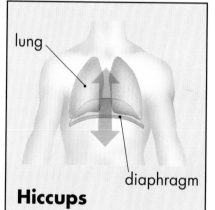

lung

diaphragm

## Hiccups

Hiccups are caused when your diaphragm contracts sharply. This stops you breathing in normally and your vocal cords make the familiar "hic" sound.

# Do it yourself

## How much air can you expel from your lungs?

**1.** You will need a large plastic container, rubber tubing, and a crayon. Fill the container with water.

**2.** Fill the sink with water and lower the container into the sink. Quickly turn it upside down without letting in any air. Push one end of the rubber tubing into the container, holding your finger over the other end to block it.

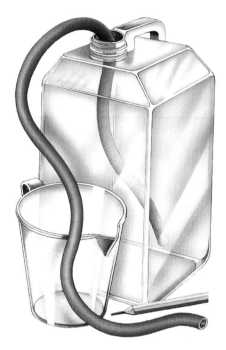

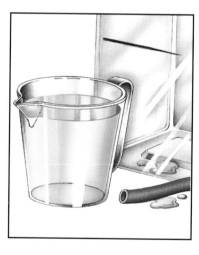

**3.** Take a deep breath and blow out through the tubing. Mark on the container the water level after you breathed out.

**4.** Empty the container and then fill it with water up to the mark. This represents the volume of air that you expelled from your lungs.

# The Nervous System

Your brain is the control center of your body. Without it, you could not move, think, or remember anything. Your brain receives information from all over your body, especially from the senses. It uses this information to coordinate your actions. The nerves carry messages from your brain to all parts of your body. The information kept in your brain for future reference is called memory. This is a record of the things you have seen, heard, and done.

The brain and spinal cord make up the central nervous system. Nerves then branch off to the rest of the body. This outer network of nerves is called the peripheral nervous system.

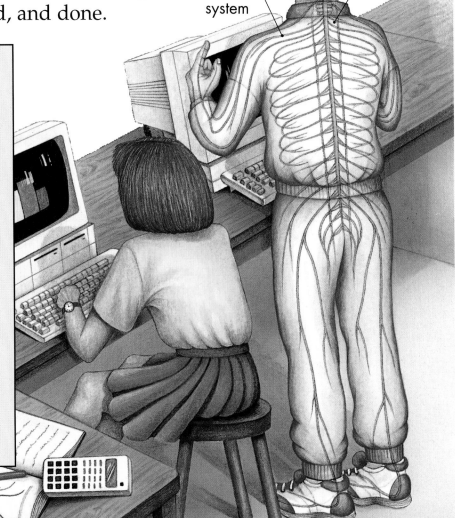

brain

spinal cord

peripheral nervous system

## 👁 Eye-Spy

Your brain determines whether you use your right or left hand for writing. Most people are right-handed, but may use the left hand for certain jobs. See which hand you use to do a variety of tasks.

# Do it yourself

**Try this test to see how fast your reflexes are.**

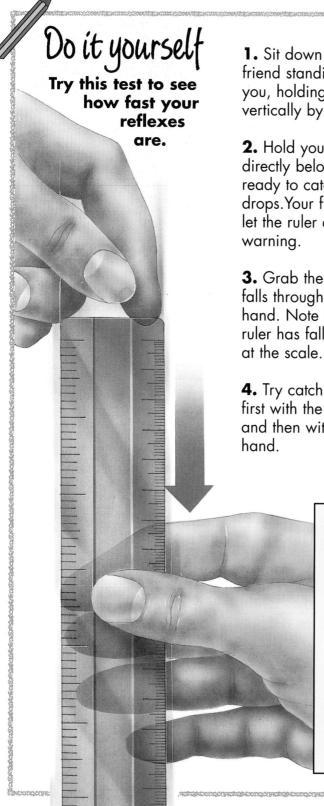

**1.** Sit down with your friend standing in front of you, holding a ruler vertically by its end.

**2.** Hold your hand open directly below the ruler, ready to catch it when it drops. Your friend should let the ruler drop without warning.

**3.** Grab the ruler as it falls through your open hand. Note how far the ruler has fallen by looking at the scale.

**4.** Try catching the ruler first with the right hand, and then with the left hand.

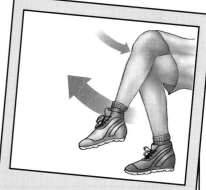

## Reflexes

Some nerves work without the brain being involved. The message rushes along a nerve to the spinal cord and the reply returns along another nerve, telling the muscle to contract. If you sit with one leg crossed over the other and somebody taps your leg just below the kneecap, the lower part of your leg kicks up. This automatic response is called a reflex.

## The Brain

The brain is a soft gray organ with a wrinkled surface, protected by the skull. It weighs about 3.3 pounds (1.5 kg) and contains as many as 10,000 million nerve cells. The spinal cord leads away from the base of the brain.

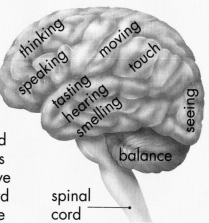

thinking
speaking
tasting
hearing
smelling
moving
touch
seeing
balance
spinal cord

21

# The Senses

The sense organs turn a stimulus, such as a touch or a noise, into an electrical message that is sent along sensory nerves to your brain. Your skin has nerve endings that are sensitive to pressure, touch, heat, and pain. Your sense of taste comes from taste buds on the tongue. It is linked to the sense of smell, which comes from sensors in your nose. Your ears hear sound waves that enter the ear and hit the eardrum. You see with your eyes. Light rays enter the front of the eye and produce a picture on the retina at the back. The picture is detected by special sensors called rods and cones.

## Balance

Ears help you to keep your balance. Inside your ears there are three tubes filled with fluid. When you move your head, the fluid moves and this sends information to your brain.

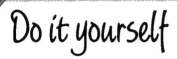

## Do it yourself

**See what happens if you eat food without being able to see or smell it.**

Blindfold a friend. Hold a piece of onion under her nose to dull her sense of smell. Now give her some food to eat. Can she tell you what she is eating? Can she tell the difference between two types of bread?

apple

potato

cheese

brown bread

white bread

When you play ball games, your senses are very important. You have to watch the ball and the other players. You have to listen for calls and be ready to move quickly.

# Do it yourself

**You can see some colors out of the corner of your eye more easily.**

**1.** Ask a friend to sit on a stool. Stand behind her. Take two pens of the same color, and hold one in each hand. Put your arms out to the side, at your friend's eye level. Slowly move your arms forward, around the front of your friend.

**2.** Ask your friend to tell you the color of the pens while keeping her eyes looking to the front.

**3.** Try with two more pens of a different color. Which color does your friend see out of the corner of her eye more easily?

## How It Works

Bright colors are more easily seen out of the corner of the eye. This is why emergency vehicles often use red and yellow—it helps them to stand out in traffic.

## Braille

Braille is a form of writing using raised dots. A blind person can feel the dots with his fingertips and translate them into words.

# The Skin

Skin provides a protective covering over your bones and muscles. It keeps out bacteria and helps to control your body temperature. The outer layer of skin, the epidermis, is made up of cells. The top cells are dead and are continually shed to be replaced by new ones from below. The epidermis protects the underlying dermis from the sun. The dermis contains many nerve endings, blood vessels, and sweat glands. Hairs grow from roots deep in the dermis.

## Skin color

Your skin helps to protect itself from the sun by producing extra melanin, the substance that gives skin its color. But using sunscreen is important, too.

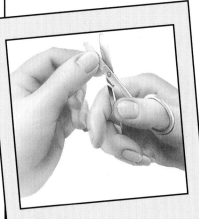

## Nails

Nails are made from tough fibers of keratin. Fingernails grow about 0.02 inch (0.05 cm) each week. If they are not cut they will continue to grow.

## Do it yourself

**Fingertips have hot and cold sensors that help you to feel temperature.**

**1.** Put warm water in a bowl, cool water in another, and ice cold water in the third.

**2.** Dip one finger in the warm water and one in the ice cold water. Wait for a minute. Can you tell the difference?

**3.** Now dip both fingers in the middle bowl. What do your fingers tell you about the temperature of the water?

When you come out of a swimming pool, the water evaporates from your skin and this makes you feel cold. The hairs on your skin stand up and you get tiny goose bumps. This helps to trap a layer of warm air around the body and makes it more difficult for heat to be lost.

nerve ending

hair
epidermis
dermis
sweat gland
blood vessel

## How It Works

When you moved your fingers into the cool bowl, your brain took a few seconds to notice that the message about temperature had changed.

## Fingerprints

Fingerprints are often used to identify people because each person's print is a unique pattern of spirals and whirls. You can take your own fingerprints by pressing your fingertips on an ink pad, then onto a piece of paper.

25

# Inheritance

Human beings vary in height, size, and color of hair, eyes, and skin. Most of your appearance is inherited from your parents. Inherited characteristics are controlled by genetic instructions, or genes. Genes are carried on chromosomes that are found in the nucleus of every cell. Most cells contain two sets of genes. One set of genes is passed from each parent to their child during reproduction. This means that you received one set of genes from your mother and one set from your father, giving you two sets of genes of your own.

There are many physical differences between individual people, even if they are of a similar age.

## Genes

Each of your parents gives you one gene for eye color. If both give you a blue eye gene, you will have blue eyes. If both give you a brown eye gene, then your eyes will be brown. But if one parent gives you a blue gene and the other a brown gene, you will have brown eyes. This is because the gene for brown eyes is stronger than the gene for blue eyes.

# Do it yourself

**Your classmates vary in height though they are all about the same age.**

**1.** Measure your longest finger. Try to measure to the point where the finger stops, rather than to the end of the fingernail.

**2.** Now measure the length of the same finger on other people in your class, making sure that you measure to the same point on all fingers.

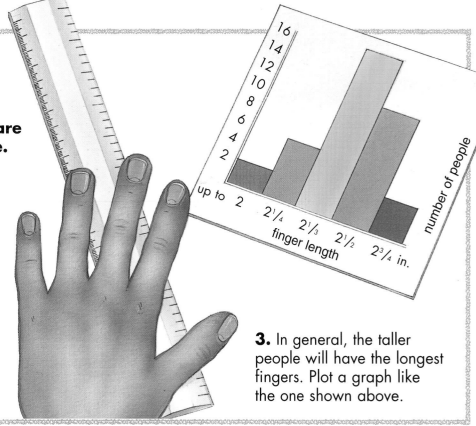

**3.** In general, the taller people will have the longest fingers. Plot a graph like the one shown above.

## Identical Twins

Identical twins are produced when a newly fertilized egg divides into two. Instead of one baby developing inside the mother's womb, two babies develop. Because they were formed from the same egg, they carry the same genes and are identical in every way.

27

# Growing Up

Some of the food that you eat helps to make you grow. The speed at which you grow depends on glands in the body. These glands make hormones that control the rate at which you use food. People do not grow steadily all the time. A baby grows rapidly, then the rate of growth slows down. It speeds up again between the ages of 11 and 14, when boys and girls start to change into men and women. Most people stop growing when they are about 20 years old.

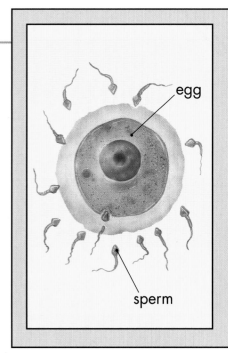

egg

sperm

 **Eye-Spy**

As people grow older, their bodies change. Old people have wrinkled skin and their limbs are stiffer. What other differences do you notice between a young and an old person?

## The Beginning of You

You started life as a tiny fertilized cell. A sperm from your father joined up with an egg in your mother's uterus. The fertilized egg then started to divide and your body organs began to form. After three months, you began to look like a miniature baby and to make your first movements. After nine months, you were fully developed and ready to be born.

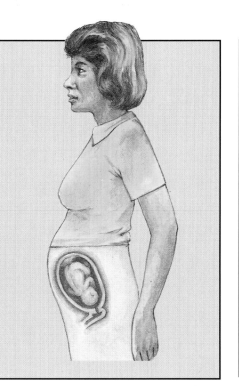

## Learning with Age

A newborn baby cannot walk, talk, or read. In the first years of life, a child learns to do these things.

One of the most important features of life is the ability to reproduce, or have babies. Human beings are different from other mammals in that their young do not lead independent lives for nearly 20 years.

# Keeping Fit

When you are fit, your body works well and you feel good. You are more energetic and less likely to suffer from illnesses such as colds or flu. Exercise keeps your muscles firm and strengthens your heart and lungs. To stay fit your body needs plenty of exercise each day. Walking, swimming, cycling, and playing sports are all good exercise. When you exercise, you use up more energy, so it is important to eat a good, balanced diet.

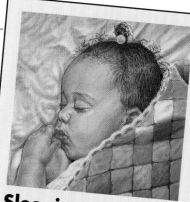

## Sleeping

Having enough sleep is essential for staying healthy. When you sleep, your heartbeat and breathing slow down, and your muscles relax.

## 👁 Eye-Spy

There are many things you can do during the day to improve your fitness, such as walking to school and taking the stairs rather than the elevator. How many other things can you think of?

## Unhealthy Lifestyle

Eating junk food and spending hours sitting in front of the television is bad for your health.

## Healthy Lifestyle

Eating plenty of fresh fruit and vegetables and exercising regularly is good for your health.

# Do it yourself

Try this simple exercise routine to see how fit you are. Take your pulse before and after the exercise. How long does it take your pulse to return to normal? As you repeat this routine each day, you should find that your recovery rate will be quicker and you will be less out of breath.

Athletes need to be very fit to perform well. They train hard for several hours each day.

**1.** To warm up, stretch your hands into the air and then bend at the waist to touch your toes five times. Bend over to each side five times.

**2.** Now start the exercises. Run on the spot for 15 seconds. Do three minutes of step-ups onto a bench. Then jump rope for two minutes.

**3.** Do 10 jumping jacks—legs apart and arms up as you jump, legs together and arms down as you land. Run on the spot for two minutes.

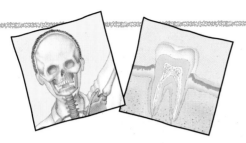

# Index

age 5, 28
arteries 16, 17

bacteria 9
bladder 14, 15
blood 5, 12, 14, 16-17, 18
blood cells 4, 16, 18
blood vessels 8, 17, 24
bones 4, 5, 6, 24
brain 4, 5, 20, 21, 22

carbon dioxide 16, 18
cartilage 5, 6, 7
cells 4, 5, 16, 17, 24, 26, 29

diaphragm 18, 19
digestion 12, 13

ears 6, 22
energy 10, 13, 18, 30
exercise 14, 16, 30-31
eyes 22, 23, 26

feces 12
fingertips 24, 25
food 5, 10-11, 12-13, 14, 16,
   18, 22, 28, 30

genes 26
glands 28
growth 12, 28

hair 4, 25, 26
heart 4, 5, 16, 17, 30
height 5, 26, 27

hiccups 18
hormones 28

intestines 12, 16

joints 6, 7

kidneys 14-15

larynx 18
ligaments 7
liver 4
lungs 4, 16, 18, 19, 30

memory 20
minerals 10
muscles 4, 6, 7, 18, 24, 30

nails 24
nerves 8, 20-21
nose 22

organs 4, 5, 6, 29
oxygen 4, 5, 16, 17, 18

platelets 17
pulse 16, 31

reflexes 21
reproduction 29

saliva 12
senses 20, 22-23
skeleton 5, 6-7
skin 4, 5, 22, 24-25

sleep 30
sperm 29
spine 6, 20, 21
stomach 12, 13
sweat 14, 24-25

teeth 8-9
temperature 4, 24
tongue 22
trachea 18

urine 14, 15

vegetarians 11
veins 16, 17
vertebrae 6
vitamins 10

wastes 14, 16
water 4, 14, 15

X rays 6